DOE/EA-1713

Environmental Assessment
for Celgard LLC
Electric Drive Vehicle Battery
and Component Manufacturing Initiative Project
Concord, NC

I0468863

April 2010

Prepared for:
Department of Energy
National Energy Technology Laboratory

National Environmental Policy Act (NEPA) Compliance
Cover Sheet

Proposed Action:
The U.S. Department of Energy (DOE) proposes, through a cooperative agreement with Celgard LLC (Celgard), to partially fund the construction of a small industrial facility (approximately 135,000 square feet) on approximately 20.6 acres of land for the manufacturing of separator materials for commercial hybrid-electric vehicle (HEV) batteries. The facility would be constructed on parcels within the International Business Park, Concord, North Carolina. This facility would support the anticipated growth in the lithium-ion battery industry and, more specifically, the HEV industry. If approved, DOE would provide approximately 50 percent of the funding for the project.

Type of Statement: Draft Environmental Assessment

Lead Agency: U.S. Department of Energy; National Energy Technology Laboratory

DOE Contact:

NEPA Information:
Jesse Garcia
NEPA Document Manager
U.S. Department of Energy
National Energy Technology Laboratory
3610 Collins Ferry Road, P.O. Box 880
Morgantown, WV 26507-0880
304-285-0256; 304-285-4403 (fax)
Jesse.Garcia@netl.doe.gov

Project Information:
Bruce Mixer
Project Manager
U.S. Department of Energy
National Energy Technology Laboratory
3610 Collins Ferry Road. P.O. Box 880
Morgantown, WV 26507-0880
304-285-4161: 304-285-4403 (fax)
Bruce.Mixer@netl.doe.gov

Abstract:
DOE prepared this Environmental Assessment (EA) to assess the potential for impacts to the human and natural environment of its Proposed Action-providing financial assistance to Celgard under a cooperative agreement. DOE's objective is to support the development of the electric drive vehicles (EDV) industry in an effort to substantially reduce the United States' consumption of petroleum, in addition to stimulating the United States' economy. More specifically, DOE's objective is to accelerate the development and production of various EDV systems by building or increasing domestic manufacturing capacity for advanced automotive batteries, their components, recycling facilities, and EDV components. This work will enable market introduction of various electric vehicle technologies by lowering the cost of battery packs, batteries, and electric propulsion systems for EDVs through high-volume manufacturing.

Under the terms of the cooperative agreement, DOE would provide approximately 50 percent of the funding for Celgard to construct a small industrial facility (approximately 135,000 square feet) on approximately 20.6 acres of land for the manufacturing of separator materials for commercial HEV batteries. The proposed project would involve the installation of a manufacturing plant with sufficient capacity to manufacture at least 1,000,000 square meters of separator material to support the assembly of at least 20,000 plug-in HEV batteries, or equivalent, per year in accordance with the requirements of DOE's Funding Opportunity Announcement. Additionally, the project would create approximately 273 permanent jobs.

The environmental analysis identified that the most notable changes, although minor, to result from Celgard's Proposed Project would occur in the following areas: air quality and greenhouse gas, noise, geology and soils, groundwater, vegetation and wildlife, socioeconomic, utilities and energy use, transportation and traffic, and human health and safety. No significant environmental effects were identified in analyzing the potential consequences of these changes.

Public Participation:
DOE encourages public participation in the NEPA process. This EA is being released for public review and comment. The public is invited to provide oral, written, or e-mail comments on this Draft EA to DOE by the close of the comment period on March 29, 2010. Copies of the Draft EA are also being distributed to cognizant Federal and State agencies. Comments received by the close of the comment period were considered in preparing the Final EA for the proposed DOE action.

TABLE OF CONTENTS

LIST OF TABLES

LIST OF FIGURES

LIST OF APPENDICES

ACRONYMS

Acronym	Definition
APE	Area of Potential Effect
AQRV	air quality related values
BMP	best management practices
CAA	Clean Air Act
CE	categorically excluded
Celgard	Celgard LLC
CEQ	Council on Environmental Quality
CFR	Code of Federal Regulations
CH_4	methane
CO	carbon monoxide
CO_2	carbon dioxide
DAQ	Division of Air Quality
dBA	decibels
DOE	U.S. Department of Energy
EA	Environmental Assessment
EDV	electric drive vehicle
EERE	Energy Efficiency and Renewable Energy
EIS	Environmental Impact Statement
EPA	U.S. Environmental Protection Agency
ESA	Environmental Site Assessment
F	Fahrenheit
FEMA	Federal Emergency Management Agency
FIRM	Flood Rate Insurance Map
FONSI	Finding of No Significant Impact
GHG	greenhouse gases
HAP	hazardous air pollutants
HEV	hybrid-electric vehicle
I	Interstate
m	meter
MeB	Mecklenburg loam, 2 to 8 percent slopes
MeD	Mecklenburg loam, 8 to 15 percent slopes
mg	milligram
mgd	million gallons per day
mtpy	metric tons per year
NAAQS	National Ambient Air Quality Standards
NCDENR	North Carolina Department of Environment and Natural Resources
NEPA	National Environmental Policy Act
NETL	National Energy Technology Laboratory
NO_2	nitrogen dioxide

Acronym	Definition
NO_x	nitrogen oxides
NPL	National Priorities List
NRIS	National Register Information System
NWI	National Wetlands Inventory
O_3	ozone
Pb	lead
PM	particulate matter
PM_{10}	particulate matter 10 microns or less
$PM_{2.5}$	particulate matter 2.5 microns or less
ppm	parts per million
PSD	prevention of significant deterioration
Recovery Act	American Recovery and Reinvestment Act of 2009, Public Law 111-5
ROD	Record of Decision
SIP	State Implementation Plan
SO_2	sulfur dioxide
std	Standard
tpy	tons per year
ug/m^3	microgram per cubic meter
U.S.	United States
U.S.C.	United States Code
USFWS	U.S. Fish and Wildlife Service
VOCs	volatile organic compounds
VT	Vehicle Technologies

This page intentionally left blank.

1.0 PURPOSE AND NEED

1.1 Background

The Department of Energy's (DOE's) National Energy Technology Laboratory (NETL) manages the research and development portfolio of the Vehicle Technologies (VT) Program for the Office of Energy Efficiency and Renewable Energy (EERE). A key objective of the VT program is accelerating the development and production of electric drive vehicle (EDV) systems to substantially reduce the United States' consumption of petroleum. Another of its goals is the development of production-ready batteries, power electronics, and electric machines that can be produced in volume economically to increase the use of EDVs.

Congress appropriated significant funding for the VT program in the American Recovery and Reinvestment Act of 2009, Public Law 111-5 (Recovery Act) to stimulate the economy and reduce unemployment in addition to furthering the existing objectives of the VT program. DOE solicited applications for this funding by issuing a competitive Funding Opportunity Announcement (DE-FOA-0000026), Recovery Act - Electric Drive Vehicle Battery and Component Manufacturing Initiative, on March 19, 2009. The announcement invited applications in seven areas of interest:

- Area of Interest 1 – Projects that would build or increase production capacity and validate production capability of advanced automotive battery manufacturing plants in the United States.
- Area of Interest 2 – Projects that would build or increase production capacity and validate production capability of anode and cathode active materials, components (e.g., separator, packaging material, electrolytes and salts), and processing equipment in domestic manufacturing plants.
- Area of Interest 3 – Projects that combine aspects of Areas of Interest 1 and 2.
- Area of Interest 4 – Projects that would build or increase production capacity and validate capability of domestic recycling or refurbishment plants for lithium-ion batteries.
- Area of Interest 5 – Projects that would build or increase production capacity and validate production capability of advanced automotive electric drive components in domestic manufacturing plants.
- Area of Interest 6 – Projects that would build or increase production capacity and validate production capability of electric drive subcomponent suppliers in domestic manufacturing plants.
- Area of Interest 7 – Projects that combine aspects of Areas of Interest 5 and 6.

The application period closed on May 19, 2009, and DOE received 119 proposals across the seven areas of interest. DOE selected 30 projects based on the evaluation criteria set forth in the funding opportunity announcement; special consideration was given to projects that promoted the objectives of the Recovery Act – job preservation or creation and economic recovery – in an expeditious manner.

This project, Celgard LLC (Celgard), was one of the 30 projects that DOE selected for funding. DOE's Proposed Action is to provide $49.3 million in financial assistance in a cost-sharing arrangement with the project proponent Celgard. The total cost of the project is estimated at $101.8 million.

1.2 Purpose and Need for Department of Energy Action

The overall purpose and need for DOE action pursuant to the VT program and the funding opportunity under the Recovery Act is to accelerate the development and production of various EDV systems by building or increasing domestic manufacturing capacity for advanced automotive batteries, recycling facilities, and EDV components, in addition to stimulating the United States' economy. This work will enable market introduction of various electric vehicle technologies by lowering the cost of battery packs, batteries, and electric propulsion systems for EDVs through high-volume manufacturing. DOE intends to further this purpose and satisfy this need by providing financial assistance under cost-sharing arrangements to this and the other 29 projects selected under this funding opportunity announcement.

This and the other selected projects are needed to reduce the United States' petroleum consumption by investing in alternative VTs. Successful commercialization of EDVs would support the DOE's Energy Strategic Goal of "protect[ing] our national and economic security by promoting a diverse supply and delivery of reliable, affordable, and environmentally sound energy." This project will also meaningfully assist in the nation's economic recovery by creating manufacturing jobs in the United States in accordance with the objectives of the Recovery Act.

1.3   National Environmental Policy Act and Related Procedures

This Environmental Assessment (EA) is prepared in accordance with the National Environmental Policy Act (NEPA), as amended (42 U.S.C 4321), the President's Council on Environmental Quality (CEQ) regulations for implementing NEPA (40 Code of Federal Regulations [CFR] 1500-1508), and DOE's implementing procedures for compliance with NEPA (10 CFR 1021). This statute and the implementing regulations require that DOE, as a Federal agency:

- Assess the environmental impacts of any Proposed Action;
- Identify adverse environmental effects that cannot be avoided, should the Proposed Action be implemented;
- Evaluate alternatives to the Proposed Action, including a No Action Alternative; and
- Describe the cumulative impacts of the Proposed Action together with other past, present, and reasonably foreseeable future actions.

These provisions must be addressed before a final decision is made to proceed with any proposed Federal action that has the potential to cause impacts to the human environment, including providing Federal funding to a project. This EA evaluates the potential individual and cumulative effects of the Proposed Project and the No Action Alternative on the physical, human, and natural environment. The EA is intended to meet DOE's regulatory requirements under NEPA and provide DOE with the information needed to make an informed decision about providing financial assistance.

NEPA requires Federal agencies to take into account the potential consequences of their actions on both the natural and human environments as part of their planning and decision-making processes. To facilitate these considerations, a number of typical actions that have been determined to have little or no potential for adverse impacts are "categorically excluded" (CE) from the detailed NEPA assessment process. Thus, the first step in determining if an action would have an adverse effect on the environment is to assess whether it fits into a defined category for which a CE is applicable. If a CE is applied, the agency prepares a Record of Categorical Exclusion to document the decision and proceeds with the action.

For actions that are not subject to a CE, the agency prepares an EA to determine the potential for significant impacts. If through the evaluation and analysis conducted for the EA process, it is determined that no significant impacts would occur as a result of the action, then the determination would result in a Finding of No Significant Impact (FONSI). The Federal agency would then publish an EA and the FONSI. The NEPA process is complete when the FONSI is executed.

If significant adverse impacts to the natural or human environment are indicated or other intervening circumstances either exist at the onset of a project or are determined through the EA process, an Environmental Impact Statement (EIS) may be prepared. An EIS is a more intensive study of the effects of the Proposed Action, and requires more rigorous public involvement. The agency formalizes its decisions relating to an action for which an EIS is prepared in a Record of Decision (ROD). Following a 30-day waiting period after publication of the Final EIS, the Agency may issue a ROD and then the NEPA process is complete.

1.4   Agency Coordination

DOE has initiated consultations with North Carolina State Historic Preservation Office, the U.S. Fish and Wildlife Service (USFWS), and the Natural Heritage Program, per requirements of Section 106 of the National Historic Preservation Act and Section 7 of the Endangered Species Act, respectively. All agency responses have been received. Copies of the agency response letters are included in Appendix A of this EA.

This page intentionally left blank.

2.0 PROPOSED ACTION AND ALTERNATIVES

2.1 Department of Energy's Proposed Action

DOE proposes, through a cooperative agreement with Celgard LLC, to partially fund the construction and establishment of a commercial-size manufacturing plant that would produce battery separator materials to be used in lithium-ion batteries. The plant would be constructed in Concord, North Carolina and would support the anticipated growth in the EDV industry and hybrid-electric vehicle industry. If approved, DOE would provide approximately 50 percent of the funding for the project.

2.2 Celgard's Proposed Project

Celgard proposes the construction of a small industrial facility (approximately 135,000 square feet) on approximately 20.6 acres of land for the manufacturing of separator materials for commercial hybrid-electric vehicle (HEV) batteries. The proposed project would involve the installation of a manufacturing plant with sufficient capacity to manufacture at least 1,000,000 square meters of separator material to support the assembly of at least 20,000 PHEV batteries, or equivalent, per year in accordance with the requirements of DOE's Funding Opportunity Announcement. The project would include warehouse space, five truck docks, and an ancillary building of approximately 5,000 square feet. The facility would include manufacturing process equipment, shipping and receiving docks and warehousing facilities, product test laboratories, quality assurance laboratories, administrative offices and common areas, maintenance shops, installation of all needed roadways and parking facilities, setting of four dry resin pellet storage silos (capacity of at least 1,000 cubic feet each), compressed air generator, and chill water systems for heating and cooling. Site preparation that would be required includes the construction of a main manufacturing building shell, employee parking lot, and commercial carrier truck access, installation of electrical feeds, city utility services (water and sewer), fire suppression lines, meters, controls valves and pumps, as needed.

One or more production lines would be installed in the new facility. Each line would consist of an extrusion line, oven line, deplier, and slitter. The quality assurance laboratory, which is currently located at the Charlotte facility, may be relocated to the new manufacturing facility. Chill water systems would be installed to provide heat and cooling. The heat transfer liquid would be approximately 13 percent propylene glycol in water in a closed loop system.

2.3 General Description and Location

The project site is located within the existing International Business Park, Concord, in Cabarrus County, North Carolina (Figure 2.2-1 and 2.2-2). The International Business Park site consists of a 517-acre master-planned business park, which was historically a combination of farmland and forest. The 20.6-acre project site, consisting of three lots (6, 7, and 8) within the business park was previously forested. The site is currently owned by two owners (CESI LLC owns lot 6 and the Nolim Group own lots 7 and 8); Celgard has entered into a Letter of Intent to purchase the lots from the two respective companies. Starting in 2008, approximately 18 acres of the site (lots 7 and 8) was cleared and rough graded for speculative development of a warehouse building by the current site owner. The grading involved extensive earthwork and recontouring of the site to provide building and related infrastructure space for a large warehouse facility. Currently, 18 acres have been rough graded and seeded to stabilize soils. The eastern portion of the site (lot 6) remains undisturbed, containing approximately 2.1 acres of early successional forest. The site is bordered by industrial use and warehouse space to the north and east, and residential properties to the southeast, south, and west.

2.4 Alternatives

DOE's alternatives to this project consist of the 45 technically acceptable applications received in response to the Funding Opportunity Announcement, Recovery Act - Electric Drive Vehicle Battery and Component Manufacturing Initiative. Prior to selection, DOE made preliminary determinations regarding the level of review

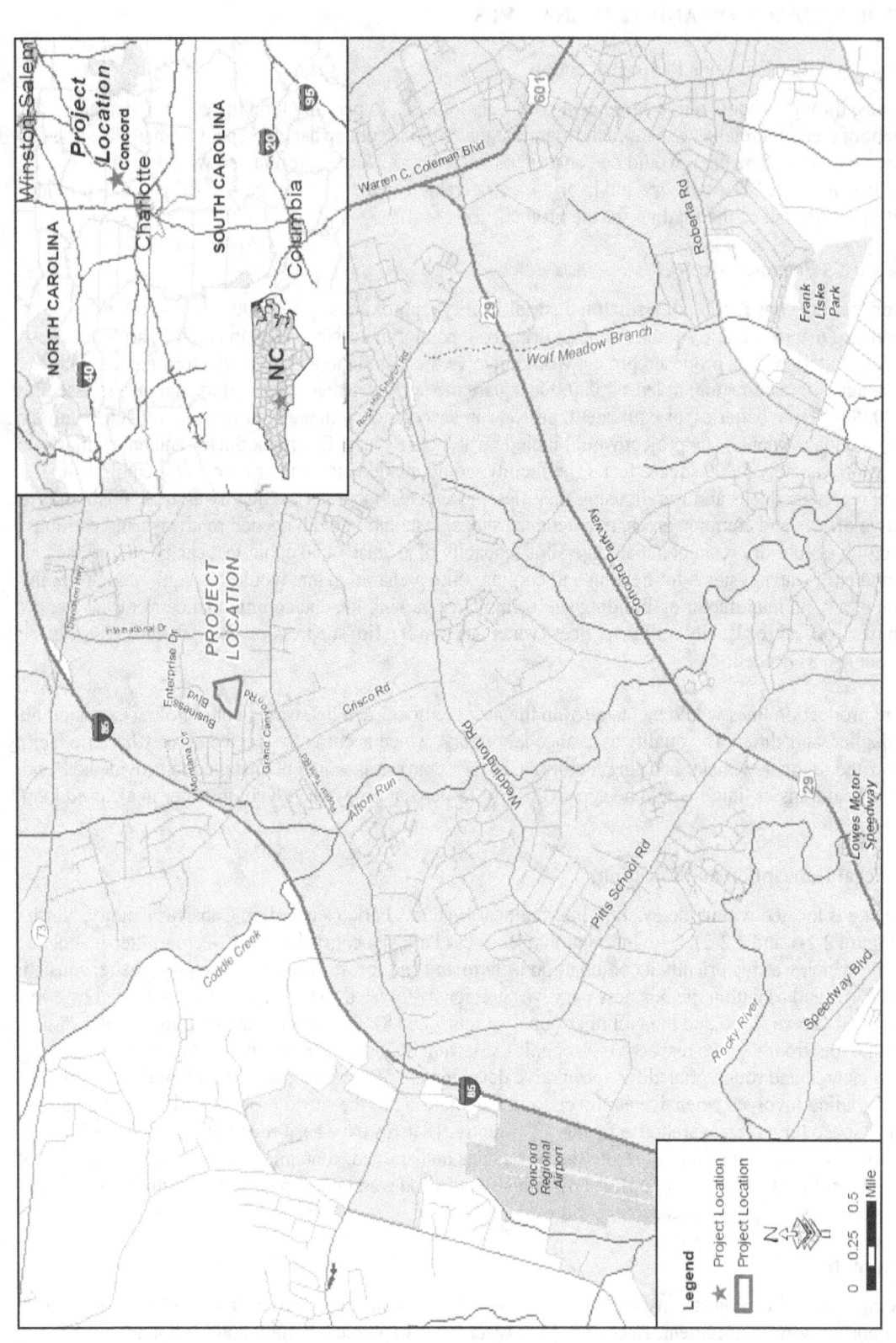

Figure 2.2-1. Regional Location Map

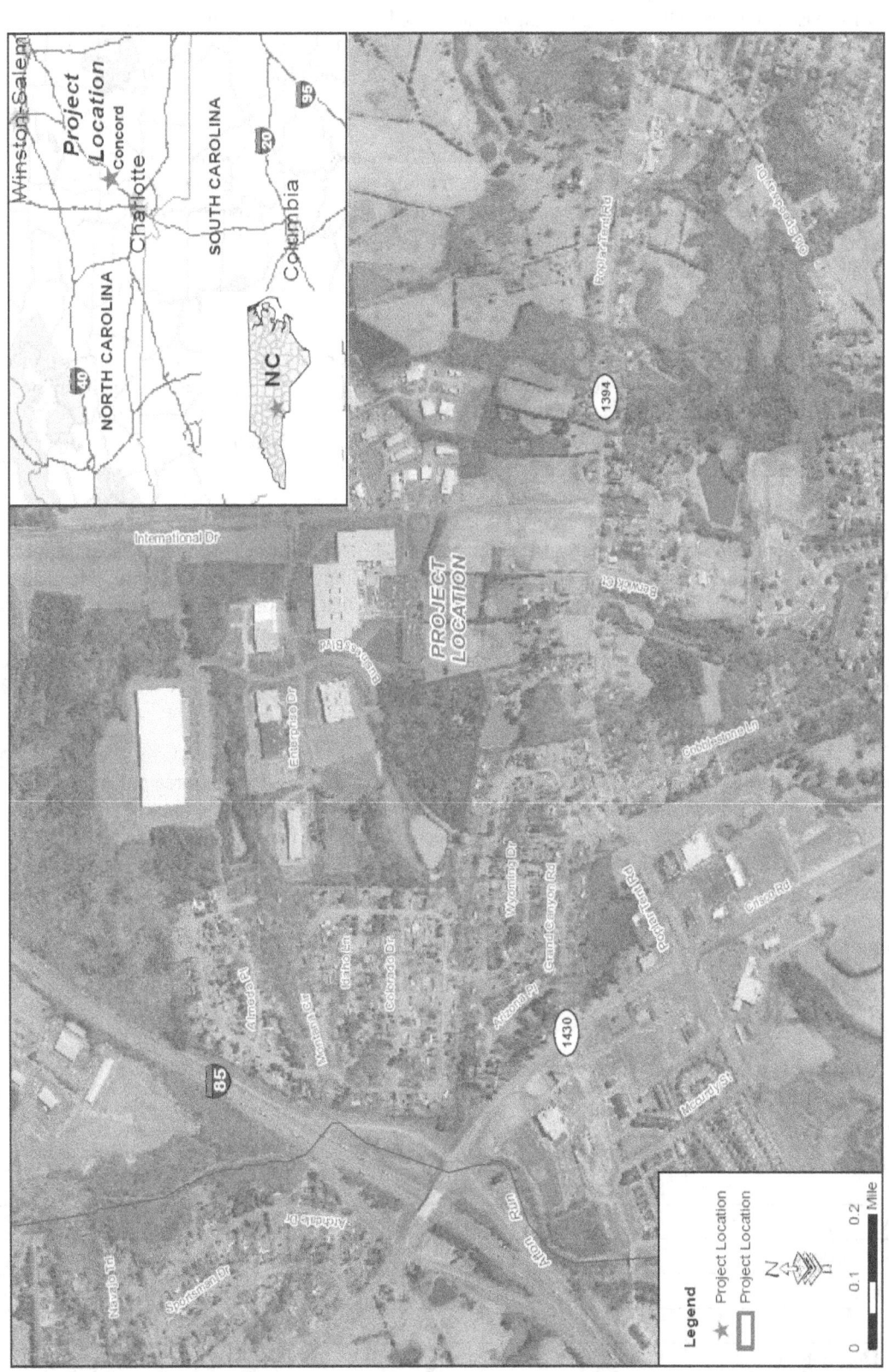

Figure 2.2-2. Site Location Map

required by NEPA based on potentially significant impacts identified in reviews of acceptable applications. A variance to certain requirements in 10 CFR 1021.216 was granted by the DOE's General Counsel. These preliminary NEPA determinations and reviews were provided to the selecting official, who considered them during the selection process.

Because DOE's Proposed Action is limited to providing financial assistance in cost-sharing arrangements to projects submitted by applicants in response to a competitive funding opportunity, DOE's decision is limited to either accepting or rejecting the project as proposed by the proponent, including its proposed technology and selected sites. DOE's consideration of reasonable alternatives is therefore limited to the technically acceptable applications and a no action alternative for each selected project.

2.5   No Action Alternative

Under the No Action Alternative, DOE would not provide funds to this proposed project. As a result, this project would be delayed while the applicant seeks other funding sources. Alternatively, the applicant would abandon this project if other funding sources are not obtained. Furthermore, acceleration of the development and production of various EDV systems would not occur or would be delayed. DOE's ability to achieve its objectives under the VT program and the Recovery Act would be reduced.

Although this and other selected projects might proceed if DOE decided not to provide financial assistance, DOE assumes for purposes of this environmental analysis that the project would not proceed without DOE assistance. If projects did proceed without DOE's financial assistance, the potential impacts would be essentially identical to those under DOE's action alternative (i.e., providing financial assistance that allows the project to proceed). In order to allow a comparison between the potential impacts of a project as implemented and the impacts of not proceeding with a project, DOE assumes that if it were to decide to withhold assistance from a project, the project would not proceed.

2.6   Alternatives Considered by Celgard

Celgard investigated numerous sites in North Carolina and neighboring states, resulting in three potential site locations. Those sites included Concord, North Carolina; Atlanta, Georgia; and Columbia, South Carolina. While all the sites met Celgard's needs for the project, the Concord site best fit the site selection screening criteria, which involved the use of an established industrial park, a recent Phase I evaluation without any issues, and a qualified and available local workforce.

2.7   Summary of Environmental Consequences

Table 2.6-1 provides a summary of the environmental, cultural, and socioeconomic impacts of the No Action and the Proposed Project.

Table 2.6-1. Summary of Environmental, Cultural, and Socioeconomic Impacts

Impact Area	No Action Alternative		Proposed Project	
	Construction	Operations	Construction	Operations
Land Use	Negligible	Negligible	Negligible	Negligible
Meteorology	Negligible	Negligible	Negligible	Negligible
Environmental Justice	Negligible	Negligible	Negligible	Negligible
Visual Resources	Negligible	Negligible	Negligible	Negligible
Surface Water	Negligible	Negligible	Negligible	Negligible
Wetlands and Floodplains	Negligible	Negligible	Negligible	Negligible
Cultural Resources	Negligible	Negligible	Negligible	Negligible

Table 2.6-1. Summary of Environmental, Cultural, and Socioeconomic Impacts (continued)

Impact Area	No Action Alternative		Proposed Project	
	Construction	Operations	Construction	Operations
Solid and Hazardous Wastes	Negligible	Negligible	Negligible	Negligible
Air Quality	Negligible	Moderate	Minor	Negligible
Greenhouse Gases	Negligible	Negligible	Minor	Beneficial
Noise	Negligible	Negligible	Minor	Minor
Geology and Soils	Negligible	Negligible	Minor	Negligible
Groundwater	Negligible	Negligible	Minor	Minor/Negligible
Vegetation and Wildlife	Negligible	Negligible	Minor	Negligible
Socioeconomics (Population and Housing)	Negligible	Negligible	Negligible	Negligible/Minor
Socioeconomics (Taxes, Revenue, Economy, Employment)	Negligible	Negligible	Minor Beneficial/Moderate Beneficial	Minor Beneficial/ Moderate Beneficial
Utilities and Energy Use	Negligible	Negligible	Minor	Negligible/Minor
Transportation and Traffic	Negligible	Negligible	Minor	Minor
Human Health and Safety	Negligible	Negligible	Negligible	Minor

This page intentionally left blank.

3.0   AFFECTED ENVIRONMENT AND ENVIRONMENTAL CONSEQUENCES

Chapter 3 provides a description of the affected environment (existing conditions) at the project site and a discussion of the environmental consequences of the No Action Alternative and the Proposed Project. Additionally, cumulative impacts and mitigation measures are discussed where appropriate. The methodology used to identify existing conditions and to evaluate potential impacts on the physical and human environment involved the following: review of the Environmental Questionnaire and the Project Narrative prepared by Celgard; review of other documentation provided by Celgard; searches of various environmental databases; agency consultations; and a site visit conducted on December 17, 2009.

3.1   Resource Areas Dismissed from Further Consideration

DOE has determined that various resources would either not be affected or would sustain negligible impacts from Celgard's Proposed Project and do not require further evaluation. They include land use, meteorology, environmental justice, visual resources, surface water, wetlands, floodplains, cultural resources, and solid and hazardous wastes; therefore, these resource areas are briefly discussed in this section of the EA and will not be evaluated further.

Land Use: The proposed project would not result in impacts to land use and zoning. According to information collected during the site visit, the land use designation for the site is Industrial. Therefore, no change in land use designation would be required under Celgard's Proposed Project.

Meteorology: Cabarrus County is characterized by a mild temperate climate. Average annual temperature ranges from lows of about 48° Fahrenheit (F) to highs of approximately 72°F. Winter months (November through February) are the coolest with average monthly low temperatures ranging from 30° to 31°F and high temperatures range from 51° to 64°F. The warmest months are the summer months of June through August. During those months, average monthly low temperatures range from 64° to 67°F and high temperatures range from 87° to 90°F. Average annual precipitation is approximately 46 inches. November is typically the driest month with average rainfall of 3.0 inches. July is typically the wettest month with an average of 5.0 inches (SERCC, 2009).

Since 1958, there have been 136 high winds events in Cabarrus County, ranging from 86 to 120 miles per hour (NCSU, 2009). In the Atlantic Ocean, hurricane season storms rarely form outside the June 1st to November 30th season. However, North Carolina's proximity to the Gulf Stream and its protruding coastline make it a likely location to receive an early season (May) spike in tropical activity. There have been two severe tropical storms reported in North Carolina; however, historical record shows that there has never been a hurricane or tropical storm in Cabarrus County. Because Cabarrus County is over 300 miles west of the North Carolina coast, it is unlikely to experience a direct hit from a hurricane. South Atlantic hurricanes usually travel north and they are extremely unlikely to travel west (NCSU, 2009). Celgard's Proposed Project would have no impact on climate, nor would climate have any impact on the action.

Environmental Justice: Celgard's Proposed Project was evaluated in accordance with EO 12898 Federal Actions Address Environmental Justice in Minority Populations and Low-Income Populations. While there are minority and low-income populations in the study area, Celgard's Proposed Project would not have a disproportionately adverse impact on these groups.

Visual Resources: The site is bordered by industrial use and warehouse space to the north and east, and residential properties to the southeast, south, and west. Impacts to identified views and vistas were determined based on an analysis of the existing quality of the landscape views, the sensitivity of the view, and the anticipated relationship of the scale and massing of the proposed buildings to the existing visual environment. Although the new construction would be noticeable, the scale and massing of the building would be consistent with the other buildings in the area. Additionally, Celgard plans to construct and maintain an earthen berm screen during the construction phrase along the southern residential boundary, which would act as both a visual and auditory barrier to the adjacent residences.

Surface Water: The project site is located within the North Carolina portion of the Yadkin-Pee Dee River basin, which drains an area of 7,221 square miles, and the Rocky River watershed (a subbasin of the Yadkin-Pee Dee River basin). The Rocky River watershed contains 1,158 linear miles of streams; major tributaries in the watershed include Irish Buffalo Creek, Goose Creek, Crooked Creek, and Coddle Creek (NC DWQ, 2008). Coddle Creek is the closest natural surface waterbody to the site (more than 1 mile to the west) and is listed as an impaired waterway for ecological/biological integrity and turbidity (i.e., water clarity) (NC DWQ, 2009). Two stormwater retention ponds are located adjacent to the site; one to the west and the other to the south.

There are no surface water features within the site; therefore, no potential exists for direct impacts to surface waters. The USFWS expressed concerns regarding impacts to any aquatic habitat, which include the removal of the riparian zone of surface waters located adjacent to the site (see Appendix A). Their review of the site, however, involved outdated aerial photographs, which did not reflect the current conditions of the site, including the extensive forest removal, which began in September of 2008. As part of the Proposed Project, no additional land would be cleared within the riparian zones of these surface water features. Landscaping of the site would further enhance the portions of riparian zone on the site that was cleared by the current land owner; therefore, impacts would be negligible.

Construction activities could cause erosion of sediments into adjacent surface water features located offsite; however, considering there are no natural surface waters nearby and there are existing stormwater retention ponds in close proximity, it is unlikely that any natural water bodies would be affected. Overall, no impacts to surface waters would be expected. Best management practices (BMPs) would be installed and maintained during land-disturbing activities to further prevent the potential of indirect impacts to surface waters from construction site runoff.

Preliminary site designs for the proposed facility show structures for the detention of stormwater; thus, it is anticipated that adequate stormwater management would be included in the design and no impacts to natural surface waters would be expected from stormwater runoff. Sediment and erosion controls would meet North Carolina Division of Water Quality requirements for the classification of watersheds. As stated previously, Coddle Creek (the closest natural surface waterbody) is listed as an impaired waterway for ecological/biological integrity and turbidity; sediment and erosion control measures, therefore, would adhere to the design standards for sensitive watersheds (15A NCAC 48 .0124).

The existing Celgard facility in Charlotte, North Carolina operates under a "No Exposure Certification for Exclusion" from National Pollutant Discharge Elimination System stormwater permitting from the North Carolina Division of Water Quality. A condition of no exposure exists at an industrial facility when all industrial materials and activities are protected by a storm resistant shelter to prevent exposure to precipitation and/or runoff. To maintain compliance with this exclusion constant oversight of activities that have the potential to cause contamination (e.g., during new equipment deliveries) is performed. Should Celgard seek this exclusion for the proposed facility, a regulatory mechanism would be in place to ensure that no contamination of site-generated stormwater would occur. No water withdrawals or discharges would occur to or from any surface waters.

Wetlands: National Wetlands Inventory (NWI) mapping does not indicate the presence of wetlands within the project site. In addition, the Cabarrus County Soil Survey did not indicate the presence of hydric soils within the project site, a potential indicator that wetlands could be present. The December 17, 2009, site visit verified no apparent wetlands were located within the project site. Two ponds which are used as stormwater retention ponds for the business park were located adjacent to the project site, one located to the west and the other to the south. No wetlands are located within the project site; therefore, no direct impacts to wetlands would occur. Indirect impacts to adjacent ponds such as sedimentation during construction would be managed and avoided through use of sediment and erosion control devices.

Floodplains: The Federal Emergency Management Agency (FEMA) Flood Insurance Rate Map (FIRM), Map Number 3710560100J does not indicate the presence of floodplain within the project site (EPA, 2009d); therefore, there would be no impacts to floodplains.

Cultural Resources: The project site is located within the existing International Business Park, Concord, in Cabarrus County, North Carolina. The International Business Park site consists of a 517-acre master-planned business park, which was historically a combination of farmland and forest. The 20.6-acre project site, consisting of three lots (6, 7, and 8) within the business park was previously forested. Starting in 2008, approximately 18 acres of the site (lots 7 and 8) was cleared and rough graded for speculative development of a warehouse building by the current site owner. The grading involved extensive earthwork and re-contouring of the site to provide building and related infrastructure space for a large warehouse facility. The eastern portion of the site (lot 6) remains undisturbed, containing approximately 2.1 acres of early successional forest.

The main geological landforms present within the project site include interfluves and hillslopes on ridges. Interfluves are characterized by a relatively undissected upland or ridge between two adjacent valleys containing streams flowing in the same general direction (NRCS, 2009). Hillslopes on ridges are characterized by relatively steeply sloping terrain (8 to 15 percent slopes). The Cabarrus County Soil Survey (NRCS, 2009) indicates two soil types within proximity to the project site that include Mecklenburg loam, 2 to 8 percent slopes (MeB) and Mecklenburg loam, 8 to 15 percent slopes (MeD).

The rough grading, of approximately 18 acres, has caused considerable disturbance to the MeB and MeD soils. During the site visit, the only area of undisturbed soils (MeB) was observed in the approximate 2.1 acres comprising lot 6. These soils were covered and stabilized by forest.

Due to the nature of the site, which contains largely disturbed soils, DOE has made a finding of No Historic Properties Effected for archeological resources in regards to this undertaking.

The Area of Potential Effects (APE) for historic structures has been determined to be ½ mile beyond the project limits. This was determined due to sight distances and present commercial, industrial, and residential building density within the surrounding community. A review of the National Register of Historic Places (NRIS, 2009) and the North Carolina GIS information available through "Google Earth" has revealed no historic resources within 1 mile of the project site, well beyond the APE for the project. A field survey confirmed that no structures 50 years or older are present within the APE for the project. On February 3, 2010, DOE received concurrence that there are no historic resources.

Solid and Hazardous Waste: The site is currently undeveloped property that has been graded to prepare the site for construction. A Phase I Environmental Site Assessment (ESA) was prepared for lots 7 and 8 of the International Business Park in March 2005 (CESI, 2005). Based on the Phase I report, no signs of a potential release are present at the site (e.g., stressed vegetation, soil staining, unusual odors) and no evidence was noted to indicate that hazardous or toxic materials are or have previously been disposed of or produced at the site (CESI, 2005). The only structure on the site is a pad-mounted transformer located in the northeast corner of lot 7. No signs of leakage from the transformer were observed (CESI, 2005). The site is not listed on the EPA's National Priority List (NPL), which designates high-priority cleanup sites under the Comprehensive Environmental Response Compensation and Liability Act, more commonly known as the Superfund Program. There are no NPL sites within at least a 3-mile radius of the site (EPA, 2009c).

Under Celgard's Proposed Project, a facility would be newly constructed at the site, which is currently vacant and graded. Solid waste and sanitary waste generated during construction activities would be limited to common construction-related waste streams. No hazardous waste would likely be generated. In-state or out-of-state landfills or recycling facilities would have the capability and capacity to accept these wastes, and therefore, there would be no impact associated with the disposal of these materials. In addition, the facility would implement BMP) to minimize the quantity of non-hazardous solid waste generated, as appropriate, during construction and to ensure proper handling of all materials. No impacts associated with the generation of construction waste would occur.

The main raw material used for operations would be polypropylene and polyethylene resins in dry pellet form. The newly constructed facility would include four dry resin storage silos of approximately 1,000 cubic feet capacity each located outdoors adjacent to the manufacturing building. In addition, the facility would store materials indoors in small containers (e.g., spray cans) to be used in the facility's battery testing laboratory that would include alcohols, solvents and electrolytes.

Based on the estimated quantity of hazardous waste to be generated (less than 200 pounds per month), the facility would be regulated as a small quantity generator of hazardous waste. Wastes would be generated primarily from quality control testing and solvent/resin mixes for process improvement operations and would include waste solvents such as alcohol and acetone as well as electrolytes (Celgard, 2009a). Celgard is making arrangements with Veolia Environmental Services, Inc., the company currently contracted by Celgard for handling its hazardous waste disposal and transport at the Charlotte, North Carolina facility (Celgard, 2009a). Approximately 22,000 pounds per year of scrap resins (polypropylene and polyethylene) would be generated and recycled offsite by Custom Polymers located in Charlotte, North Carolina (Celgard, 2009b). Once operational, the facility estimates it would generate approximately 60,000 pounds of solid municipal waste annually that would be sent offsite for disposal at a permitted landfill (Celgard, 2009a). Hazardous and non-hazardous wastes expected to be generated would be accepted for recycling or for treatment and disposal by offsite vendors; therefore, no impacts associated with the generation of operational wastes would occur.

Construction and operational waste materials would be sent off site for recycling, or treated and disposed of at a disposal facility or landfill. During construction, preventative measures such as providing fencing around the construction site, establishing contained storage areas, providing stormwater runoff protection and sediment erosion protection, and controlling the flow of construction equipment and personnel would reduce the potential for a release to occur. In the event that a release occurs, immediate action would be taken to contain and clean up the released material in accordance with Federal, state, and local regulations.

3.2   Resource Areas Considered Further

Environmental resource areas carried through for further consideration of the potential impact of Celgard's Proposed Project include air quality, greenhouse gas, noise, geology and soils, groundwater, vegetation and wildlife, socioeconomics, utilities and energy use, transportation and traffic, and human health and safety.

3.2.1   Air Quality and Greenhouse Gas

Air Quality Management

The purpose of the air quality analysis is to determine whether emissions from a proposed new or modified source of air pollution, in conjunction with emissions from existing sources, would cause or contribute to the deterioration of the air quality in the area. The Clean Air Act (CAA) requires the U.S. Environmental Protection Agency (EPA) to set National Ambient Air Quality Standards (NAAQS) for pollutants considered harmful to public health and the environment. NAAQS include two types of air quality standards (40 CFR 50.1(e)). Primary standards protect public health, including the health of sensitive populations such as asthmatics, children, and the elderly. Secondary standards protect public welfare, including protection against decreased visibility, damage to animals, crops, vegetation, and buildings. EPA has established NAAQS for six principal pollutants, which are called "criteria pollutants": ozone (O_3), carbon monoxide (CO), nitrogen dioxide (NO_2), particulate matter (PM) (particulate matter 10 microns or less [PM_{10}], particulate matter 2.5 microns or less [$PM_{2.5}$]), sulfur dioxide (SO_2), and lead (Pb). A state's air quality regulations may further regulate concentrations of the criteria pollutants. Table 3.2.1-1 lists the NAAQS and North Carolina AAQS.

Table 3.2.1-1. National and North Carolina Ambient Air Quality Standards

Pollutant	Standard	Averaging Time	Standard Type
Carbon Monoxide	35 ppm (40 mg/m³)	1-hour	Primary
	9 ppm (10 mg/m³)	8-hour	
Lead	0.15 µg/m³	Rolling 3-Month Average[1]	Primary and Secondary
	1.5 µg/m³	Quarterly Average	
Nitrogen Dioxide	0.053 ppm (100 µg/m³)	Annual (Arithmetic Mean)	Primary and Secondary
PM$_{10}$	150 µg/m³	24-hour	Primary and Secondary
PM$_{2.5}$	35 µg/m³	24-hour	Primary and Secondary
	15.0 µg/m³	Annual (Arithmetic Mean)	
Ozone	0.12 ppm	1-hour[2]	Primary and Secondary
	0.075 ppm (2008 std)	8-hour[3]	
	0.08 ppm (1997 std)	8-hour[4]	
Sulfur Dioxide	0.5 ppm (1300 µg/m³)	3-hour	Secondary
	0.14 ppm	24-hour	Primary
	0.03 ppm	Annual (Arithmetic Mean)	
Total Suspended Particulates[5]	75 µg/m³	Annual (Arithmetic Mean)	Primary and Secondary
	150 µg/m³	24-hour	

(1) Final rule signed October 15, 2008.
(2) As of June 15, 2005. 1-hour O$_3$ was revoked in all areas except 14 8-hour O$_3$ nonattainment Early Action Compact Areas. Cabarrus County, North Carolina is not an Early Action Compact Area.
(3) As of September 16, 2009, EPA is reconsidering its 2008 decision for setting new national standards for 8-hr ground level ozone.
(4) The 1997 standard and its implementation rules would remain in place as EPA undertakes rulemaking to address the transition to the 2008 standard.
(5) North Carolina AAQS
µg/m³ – microgram/per cubic meter; mg – milligram; ppm – parts per million; std – standard.
Source: EPA, 2009a, NCDENR, 2009

To determine compliance with the NAAQS, emissions of criteria pollutants from a new or modified source(s) are modeled to determine their air dispersion concentrations. In addition to the six criteria pollutants outlined in the CAA, several other substances raise concerns with regard to air quality and are regulated through the CAA Amendments of 1990. These substances include hazardous air pollutants (HAPs), and toxic air pollutants such as metals, nitrogen oxides (NO$_X$), and volatile organic compounds (VOCs). NO$_X$ and VOCs are precursors for O$_3$.

Areas that meet the air quality standard for the criteria pollutants are designated as being in attainment. Areas that do not meet the air quality standard for one or more of the criteria pollutants are designated as being in nonattainment for that standard. The CAA requires nonattainment states to submit to the EPA a State Implementation Plan (SIP) for attainment of the NAAQS (40 CFR 51.166, 40 CFR 93). Maintenance areas are those that at one point had not met the NAAQS but are currently maintaining the standards through the requirements in the SIP.

The 1990 Amendments to the CAA require Federal actions to show conformance with the SIP. Federal actions are those projects that are funded by Federal agencies and include the review and approval of a Proposed Action through the NEPA process. Conformance with the SIP means conformity to the approved SIP's purpose of eliminating or reducing the severity and number of violations of the NAAQS, and achieving expeditious attainment of such standards (40 CFR 51 and 93). The need to demonstrate conformity is applicable only to nonattainment and maintenance areas.

Class I Areas and Sensitive Receptors
For areas that are already in compliance with the NAAQS, the Prevention of Significant Deterioration (PSD) requirements provide maximum allowable increases in concentrations of pollutants, which are expressed as increments (40 CFR 52.21). Allowable PSD increments currently exist for three pollutants: SO$_2$, NO$_2$, and PM$_{10}$ (Table 3.2.1-2).

Table 3.2.1-2. Allowable Prevention of Significant Deterioration Increments ($\mu g/m^3$)

Pollutant--Averaging Period	Class I Area	Class II Area
SO_2--3-Hour	25	512
--24-Hour	5	91
--Annual	2	20
NO_2--Annual	2.5	25
PM_{10}--24-Hour	8	30
--Annual	4	17

$\mu g/m^3$ – microgram/per cubic meter.
Source: 40 CFR 52.21(c)

One set of allowable increments exists for Class II areas, which covers most of the United States and another set of more stringent allowable increments exists for Class I areas. Because of their pristine environment, Class I areas require more rigorous safeguards to prevent deterioration of their air quality. For the purposes of PSD review, the Federal government has identified mandatory Class I areas, which as defined in the CAA, are the following that were in existence as of August 7, 1977: national parks over 6,000 acres, national wilderness areas and national memorial parks over 5,000 acres, and international parks (NPS, 2009a). In general, proposed projects that are within 62 miles (100 kilometers) of Class I areas must evaluate impacts of the project on air quality related values (AQRVs) such as visibility, flora/fauna, water quality, soils, odor, and any other resources specified by the Federal Land Manager (NPS, 2009b).

Areas that are not in attainment with the NAAQS are subject to the Nonattainment New Source Review. Overall, for the purposes of air quality analysis, any area to which the general public has access is considered a sensitive receptor site, and includes residences, day care centers, educational and health facilities, places of worship, parks, and playgrounds.

Greenhouse Gases

Greenhouse gases (GHGs) are pollutants of concern for air quality and climate change. GHGs include water vapor, carbon dioxide (CO_2), methane (CH_4), NO_X, O_3, and several chlorofluorocarbons. Water vapor is a naturally occurring GHG and accounts for the largest percentage of the greenhouse effect. Next to water vapor, CO_2 is the second-most abundant GHG and is typically produced from human-related activities. The largest source of CO_2 emissions globally is the combustion of fossil fuels such as coal, oil, and gas in power plants, automobiles, industrial facilities and other sources. Additionally, a number of specialized industrial production processes and product uses such as mineral production, metal production and the use of petroleum-based products can also lead to CO_2 emissions. The manufacturing of lithium-ion battery separator material could produce CO_2 emissions.

Although regulatory agencies are taking actions to address GHG effects, there are currently no state or Federal standards or regulations limiting CO_2 emissions and concentrations in the ambient air. In response to the *FY2008 Consolidated Appropriations Act* (H.R. 2764; Public Law 110–161), EPA issued the *Final Mandatory Reporting of Greenhouse Gases Rule* (GHG Reporting Rule), which became effective January 1, 2010. The GHG Reporting Rule requires annual reporting of GHG emissions to EPA from large sources and suppliers in the United States, including suppliers of fossil fuels or industrial GHGs; manufacturers of vehicles and engines; and facilities that emit greater than 25,000 metric tons per year (mtpy) (27,558 tons per year [tpy]) each of CO_2 and other GHGs. The intent of the rule is to collect accurate and timely emissions data to inform future policy decisions and programs to reduce emissions, as well as fight against the effects of climate change.

Additionally, on September 30, 2009, EPA proposed, under the CAA New Source Review and Title V operating permit programs, new GHG thresholds that would trigger review and permitting. This proposed requirement would cover nearly 70 percent of the nation's largest stationary source GHG emitters (including power plants, refineries, and cement production facilities), while shielding small businesses and farms from permitting requirements. Congress is currently reviewing the proposed thresholds and requirements are currently being reviewed by Congress.

3.2.1.1   Affected Environment

Air Quality

The North Carolina Department of Environment and Natural Resources (NCDENR), Division of Air Quality (DAQ), which is responsible for monitoring air quality for each of the criteria pollutants and assessing compliance, has also promulgated rules governing ambient air quality in the State of North Carolina. These rules are codified in North Carolina Air Quality Rules, 15A NCAC 2D.0400. Cabarrus County is part of the Charlotte-Gastonia-Rock Hill moderate nonattainment for the 1997 8-hour O_3 standard. Additionally, NCDENR recommended that the county be designated as nonattainment for the 2008 8-hr O_3 standard (EPA, 2009b).

Because Concord, North Carolina is within the Cabarrus County nonattainment area, Federal actions within Concord, North Carolina must show conformity with the SIP, and Celgard's Proposed Project would fall under the General Conformity Rule; however, for this EA, DOE would not need to demonstrate SIP conformity because under the General Conformity Rule, Federal actions within moderate nonattainment areas, do not have to demonstrate conformity if their total direct and indirect emissions would be less than 100 tpy for all criteria pollutants, except VOC (50 tpy) and Pb (25 tpy) (40 CFR 93, Subpart B). The section below provides further discussions on the current and projected emissions from the Celgard facility.

Current Air Emissions

There is currently no process operations conducted at the Concord site by Celgard; therefore, Celgard does not have any sources that emit air pollutants and does not have an air quality permit.

3.2.1.2   Environmental Consequences

3.2.1.2.1   No Action Alternative

The No Action Alternative is treated in this EA as the "No-Build" Alternative. That is, under the No Action Alternative, Celgard would not construct and operate a commercial lithium-ion battery separator manufacturing facility at the Concord facility because of the absence of DOE funding assistance.

With the No Action Alternative, DOE would not fully meet its goal for supporting United States based manufacturing to produce advanced EDV batteries and components. With reduced DOE funding, industries may be less willing to invest in the advanced technology that would help increase production of these batteries, especially the lithium-ion batteries and their components. Because of the greater energy density and lighter weight than other batteries, lithium batteries are proving to be most promising for the commercial viability of electric vehicles (DOE, 2001). Without alternative fuel sources for automobiles, the United States will continue its dependence on and consumption of petroleum and other fossil fuels; consequentially, the current trends of increased CO_2 concentrations in the Earth's atmosphere will continue, increasing the effect on climate change.

3.2.1.2.2   Proposed Project

Construction

The Celgard facility, which would include the main building, employee parking lot, commercial carrier truck access, installation of electrical feeds, city utility services (water and sewer), fire suppression lines, meters, controls valves and pumps, would be constructed on 20.6 acres of land. Rough grading and earthwork has occurred on 18 acres of the land by the current owner. Celgard plans to finalize the grading on the remainder of the land during the construction phase.

During construction, the equipment used to construct the proposed facilities would intermittently emit quantities of five criteria air pollutants: CO, NO_X, SO_2, PM_{10}, and VOC. In addition to tailpipe emissions from heavy equipment, ground surface disturbances during excavation and grading activities could potentially generate fugitive dust. Fugitive dust, such as dirt stirred up from construction sites, can affect both environmental and public health. The type and severity of the effects depend in large part on the size and nature of the dust particles. The types of effects that can occur to humans include inhalation of fine particles that can then accumulate in the respiratory system causing various respiratory problems including persistent coughs, wheezing, eye irritations, and physical discomfort.

Exhaust emissions from equipment used in construction, coupled with likely fugitive dust emissions, could cause minor, short-term degradation of local air quality. DOE expects the overall impacts to air quality from the construction of the proposed facility would be short-term and minor.

Operations
One or more production lines would be installed in the new facility. Each line would consist of an extrusion line, oven line, deplier, and slitter. Based on the type of equipment being proposed for use at the facility, Celgard would use the dry process method to manufacture lithium-ion battery separator. The dry process involves melting a polyolefin resin, extruding it into a film, thermally annealing it to increase the size and amount of the material's crystalline structure, and precisely stretching it to form tightly ordered micropores (Arora and Zhang, 2004). The dry process uses no solvents and does not involve combustion in the process (Arora and Zhang, 2004). Because there is no chemical reaction or combustion involved in the process, no emissions would be generated from operations of the proposed Celgard facility. The facility would not be required to obtain an air quality permit.

There are eight Federal mandatory Class I areas within North Carolina and surrounding states for which the NCDENR requires a PSD review to determine potential impact; however, none of these areas are within 62 miles (100 kilometers) of the proposed project site. Therefore, a PSD increment and AQRV analysis for Class I area would not be required. All other areas within North Carolina's border are designated as Class II. Sensitive receptors within 1 mile of the proposed project site include several homes, a school, and one church, with two additional churches within 1.3 miles (EPA, 2009c). The air quality would not be affected for these sensitive receptors because the facility would not emit any air pollutant.

Overall, no adverse impacts to air quality are expected to occur at the Celgard Concord site as a result of the proposed project.

Carbon Footprint
North Carolina continues to experience increases in GHG emissions at a rate faster than the nation as a whole. In 2000, on a gross emissions consumption basis (i.e., excluding carbon sinks), North Carolina accounted for approximately 180 million metric tons of CO_2 emissions, an amount equal to 2.5 percent of total United States GHG emissions. From 1990 to 2000, North Carolina's gross GHG emissions were up 33 percent, while national gross emissions rose by 17 percent, during this period. While North Carolina forests are a net carbon sink, the principal sources of North Carolina's GHG emissions are electricity use (including electricity imports) and transportation, accounting for 42 percent and 29 percent of North Carolina's gross GHG emissions in 2000, respectively (CCS, 2007).

Although the facility would be responsible for CO_2 emissions, this would be as a result of energy consumption and not production directly from the facility's processes. The Celgard facility would have no reporting requirements under the *Final Mandatory Reporting of Greenhouse Gases Rule*, which became effective on January 1, 2010, because the Celgard facility would not directly emit at least 25,000 mtpy of CO_2 from its processes. Implementation of the proposed project would not trigger the facility's compliance with this rule.

The manufacture of EDV batteries and components would increase production of EDVs in the United States. Electric vehicles emit no tailpipe pollutants. Therefore, they can provide significant air-quality benefits to targeted regions (DOE, 1999). Overall, there would be beneficial impacts on climate change as Celgard's Proposed Project, would help the viability of the commercial market for EDVs; thereby reducing the carbon footprint of the transportation sector.

3.2.1.3   Cumulative Impacts

Other than the proposed project at the Celgard facility, no other projects are planned. No reasonably foreseeable actions have been identified that would interact with the Proposed Action to generate cumulative adverse impacts to air quality.

3.2.1.4   Proposed Mitigation Measures

During construction, typical mitigation measures to minimize air quality issues caused by fugitive dust and tailpipe emissions would include the following:

- Require all construction crews and contractors to comply with the state regulations for fugitive dust control during construction.
- Maintain the engines of construction equipment according to manufacturers' specifications.
- Minimize the idling of equipment while the equipment is not in use.
- Implement reasonable measures, such as applying water to exposed surfaces or stockpiles of dirt, when windy or dry conditions promote problematic fugitive dust emissions. Adhering to these BMPs would minimize any fugitive dust emissions. Adhering to mitigation measures and BMPs would reduce the adverse impacts from fugitive dust emissions.

No mitigation measures would be required during operations at the Celgard facility, because operations at the facility would not generate air pollution.

3.2.2   Noise

3.2.2.1   Affected Environment

The proposed site is located within the existing International Business Park and consists of three lots (6, 7, and 8). These lots were previously forested, however, approximately 18 acres of the 20.6-acre site was cleared and roughly graded in 2008, in preparation for the construction of a large warehouse by the current owner. The property is zoned Industrial, and is currently bordered by industrial use and warehouse space to the north and east, and residential properties to the south, west, and southeast.

The nearest sensitive receptors to the site are the residential properties located to the south, west, and southeast of the property. The nearest homes are those located directly adjacent to the southern border of the project site located on Grand Canyon Road; those located approximately 300 yards to the west of the site on Montana Circle; and those located approximately 300 yards to the southeast off Poplar Tent Road. The nearest school is approximately 0.7 miles northwest of the site, across Interstate 85 (I-85), with the next closest school at 2.5 miles to the east. The nearest three churches are located southeast of the site, with the closest at about 1 mile and the other two at about 1.3 miles. The nearest hospital is about 2.8 miles to the northeast (EPA, 2009c).

The site is located within the vicinity of various existing noise sources that contribute to the baseline noise level. I-85 is within approximately 0.6 miles to the west of the site at its closest point. Davidson Highway (Highway 73) is approximately 1.2 miles to the north of the site, and Warren C. Coleman Boulevard (Highway 601 Bypass) is approximately 2.5 miles east of the site. Concord Regional Airport is located about 3 miles to the southwest of the site. Lowes Motor Speedway is about 3.5 miles south of the site. Furthermore, the International Business Park is populated with various other industrial facilities. Most manufacturing operations are contained indoors; however, each facility emits normal noise related to truck and employee traffic and building mechanical systems such as blowers, heating, ventilation, and air conditioning units, etc.

3.2.2.2   Environmental Consequences

3.2.2.2.1   No Action Alternative

Under the No Action Alternative, plant construction and operation would not occur; therefore, no impacts would occur regarding noise levels.

3.2.2.2.2   Proposed Project

Construction

Short-term but measurable adverse minor impacts to noise levels are expected during the construction phase of the proposed Celgard facility. Site preparation and construction would include final grading of the property, construction of the main manufacturing building shell and all internal structural configurations, needed roadways and employee parking lot, commercial carrier truck access and loading docks, installation of utility lines, and installation of all manufacturing and other facility equipment. Increases in ambient noise levels during construction would mainly result from the use of heavy construction equipment and delivery trucks. The typical noise levels from any construction site would be expected to be within the range of 75 to 90 decibels (dBA). Construction noise levels onsite would primarily be limited to the immediate vicinity of the project site and would be short-term and intermittent.

The construction activities of Celgard's Proposed Project are expected to last for approximately 11 to 12 months (Celgard, 2009a). Construction of Celgard's Proposed Project is expected to utilize approximately 80 to 100 workers during the three-month peak phase of construction and approximately 40 to 60 workers during the remaining eight to nine months. The personal vehicles of these construction workers would contribute to regional noise levels during this period, primarily at the beginning and ending of the workday.

It is likely that due to their proximity, the nearby residences would be temporarily disturbed by the construction noise. To mitigate noise disturbance to the adjacent homes along the southern residential boundary, Celgard plans to construct and maintain an earthen berm screen during the construction phase to act as an auditory and visual barrier. All construction activities would abide by the Cabarrus County Noise Ordinance, which limits building operations in a residential or business district to the hours between 7:00 a.m. and 9:00 p.m. on Monday through Saturday, and between 1:00 p.m. and 9:00 p.m. on Sunday (Cabarrus County, 2009a).

Operations

The main sources of noise during operations would be from the typical building mechanical equipment (heating, ventilation, and air conditioning systems) and from the truck and personal-vehicle traffic accessing the facility. All equipment directly involved in product manufacturing would be located indoors. The only operation occurring partially outdoors would be the truck loading dock area.

Celgard's Proposed Project would generate a minor long-term increase in noise due to truck and personal-vehicle traffic into and out of the business park. The operations would be expected to require approximately four truck visits per day for deliveries and shipments, and roughly 150 personal vehicle visits per day due to the approximately 273 employees (including plant shift workers and office staff). The plant would operate 24 hours per day with three shifts. Approximately 80 employees would work per shift (Celgard, 2009a).

Because this facility would be located within an existing industrial business park that currently contains numerous other industrial facilities with mechanical and traffic-related noises, any increase in ambient noise levels resulting from operations of Celgard's Proposed Project would be minor. Furthermore, there are other existing comparable and louder noise sources in the vicinity, including existing truck traffic, major highways, an airport, and a motor speedway. To mitigate the operational and visual disturbance to the nearby residences, Celgard would maintain an earthen berm screen along the southern residential boundary, as previously discussed.

3.2.2.3   Cumulative Impacts

Other than the proposed Celgard project, no other projects are planned. The proposed Celgard project would generate minor impacts that would contribute to cumulative noise impacts associated with the historical trend of past, present, and reasonable foreseeable future activities. Noise emissions could have a minor cumulative impact when occurring with other existing noises.

3.2.2.4   Proposed Mitigation Measures

Celgard's Proposed Project includes the construction and maintenance of an earthen berm screen along the southern border of the property to reduce noise and visual disturbance to the nearby residences. All Celgard construction and operations associated with this project would abide by the noise guidelines documented in the Cabarrus County Noise Ordinance (Cabarrus County, 2009a).

3.2.3   Geology and Soils

The main geological landforms present within the project site include interfluves and hillslopes on ridges. Interfluves are characterized by a relatively undissected upland or ridge between two adjacent valleys containing streams flowing in the same general direction (NRCS, 2009). Hillslopes on ridges are characterized by relatively steeply sloping terrain (8 to 15 percent slopes). The Cabarrus County Soil Survey (NRCS, 2009) indicates two soil types within proximity to the project site, which include MeB, 2 to 8 percent slopes and MeD, 8 to 15 percent slopes. Table 3.2.3-1 contains the properties of each soil unit and their respective geological landform.

Table 3.2.3-1. Study Area Soils

Soil Unit	Geologic Landform	Slope (percent)	Flooding Frequency	Hydric Rating	Commercial Building Construction
MeB	Interfluves	2-8	None	Not hydric	Somewhat limited
MeD	Hillslopes on Ridges	8-15	None	Not hydric	Very limited

Source: NRCS, 2009

As shown in Table 3.2.3-1, soils within the project site are not prone to flooding. A "none" frequency rating means that flooding is not probable; the chance of flooding is nearly 0 percent in any year and flooding occurs less than once in 500 years. No mapped hydric soils occur within the project site.

Overall, soils within the project site are somewhat to very limited for commercial building construction (e.g., structures typically less than three stories high and lacking basements). The construction ratings are based on the soil properties that affect the capacity of the soil to support a load without movement and on the properties that affect excavation and construction costs (i.e., depth to a water table, ponding, flooding, subsidence, shrink-swell potential, and compressibility). "Somewhat limited" indicates that the soil has features that are moderately favorable for the specified use and limitations can be overcome or minimized by special planning, design, or installation. In addition, fair performance and moderate maintenance can be expected. "Very limited" indicates that the soil has one or more features that are unfavorable for the specified use. The limitations generally cannot be overcome without major soil reclamation, special design, or expensive installation procedures. Poor performance and high maintenance can be expected. MeB soils are somewhat limited for commercial building construction due to shrink swell potential and MeD soils are very limited for commercial building construction due to steep slopes (NRCS, 2009).

The December 17th, 2009, site visit of the study area revealed the majority of the project site (approximately 18 acres) has been rough graded by the current property owner within the past year. The rough grading has caused considerable disturbance to the soils. Approximately 18 acres of both MeB and MeD soils have been graded and leveled. Within these areas, a large area of exposed soil was observed; however, contractors hired by the existing land owner have stabilized the site through placement of seeding and hay. In addition, silt fencing was observed in downslope areas to control sediment erosion and to prevent sediment transport into adjacent ponds located to the west and south of the project site. The only area of undisturbed soils (MeB) was observed in the approximate 2.1 acres comprising lot 6. These soils were covered and stabilized by forest.

3.2.3.1.1 No Action Alternative

Under the No Action Alternative, plant construction and operations would not occur; therefore, no additional impacts would occur to existing geology and soil resources.

3.2.3.1.2 Proposed Project

Construction

Under Celgard's Proposed Project, a direct permanent adverse impact would occur to the remaining 2.1 acres of undisturbed soils associated with lot 6 of the project site. In addition, final contouring and stabilization would be required for the approximate 18 acres of the remaining project site, which has been rough graded. Once final grading has occurred, the proposed facility would require paving and establishment of impervious surface to support the facility and associated infrastructure (i.e., entrance roads, parking, and stormwater management). These impacts, however, would be localized and minor. BMPs such as sediment control devices and seeding or sodding of temporarily disturbed areas following construction would reduce the potential for adverse indirect impacts such as soil erosion. As stated within Section 3.3.4, MeD soils within the study area of the proposed facility are very limited for commercial building construction due to steep slopes. This constraint, however, has been previously addressed by the existing property owner through the extensive grading and leveling of the site. Undisturbed portions of lot 6 are located within MeB soils, which would require minor grading.

Operations

Operations of the site would have no impacts to either geology or soil resources. Manufacturing would occur within the facility and the product would be transferred offsite using existing road infrastructure.

3.2.3.2 Cumulative Impacts

Industrial and rural farm and residential uses adjacent to the project site have caused localized and adverse disturbances to soils. As the project site is located within a State- and locally-approved business park, additional disturbances would likely occur to soils within the remaining undeveloped lots located in the business park as they become developed. These impacts would be localized, and disturbance would occur over time. Therefore, overall adverse cumulative impacts to soils and geology would be minor.

3.2.3.3 Proposed Mitigation Measures

Soils would be stabilized following construction to minimize erosion and offsite impacts.

3.2.4 Groundwater

3.2.4.1 Affected Environment

The project site is located in the Piedmont physiographic province, which occurs in the middle portion of the State with the Coastal Plain to the east and the Blue Ridge Mountains to the west. The groundwater system in the Piedmont region is essentially a two-part system comprised of water-bearing regolith (i.e., the layer of loose rock and soil resting on bedrock) and the underlying bedrock, which contains water-filled fractures. Precipitation infiltrates the surface soil and regolith until it reaches the zone of saturation, where it is stored as groundwater. Where regolith is very thin, the saturated zone may be entirely contained in fractured bedrock (LeGrand, Sr., 2004). Throughout most of the Piedmont, groundwater wells yield an average of 18 to 21 gallons per minute (Huffman, 1996).

3.2.4.2 Environmental Consequences

3.2.4.2.1 No Action Alternative

Under the No Action Alternative, construction and operations would not occur; therefore, no impacts would occur to groundwater.

3.2.4.2.2 Proposed Project

Construction

The project proponent would use BMPs to guide the avoidance, minimization, and response to pollutant spills that could affect groundwater during construction. Nevertheless, there is potential for minor groundwater contamination to occur.

Operations

Standard Operating Procedures, BMPs, or plans would be developed and adhered to during operations of the facility for the safe handling of materials, and there would be procedures to follow in the event of a spill. Nevertheless, there is a potential for minor groundwater contamination to occur. No groundwater withdrawals would be proposed; therefore, no impacts on groundwater levels would occur.

3.2.4.3 Cumulative Impacts

Currently, other than the proposed Celgard project, no other projects are planned. However, the project site is located within a State- and locally-approved business park; therefore, it is anticipated that with the full development of the business park, cumulative effects would include a greater potential for groundwater contamination to occur, which could be associated with increased activity in the area.

3.2.4.4 Proposed Mitigation Measures

No mitigation measures would be required for groundwater.

3.2.5 Vegetation and Wildlife

3.2.5.1 Affected Environment

3.2.5.1.1 Vegetation

The December 17, 2009, site visit of the study area revealed the majority of the project site (approximately 18 acres) has been rough graded by the current property owner within the past year and contains barren soil. Approximately 2.1 acres of early successional forest was located on lot 6 of the project site. This forest stand had a combination of red cedar (*Juniperus virginiana*), tuliptree (*Liriodendron tulipfera*), black locust (*Robinea pseudoacacia*) and willow oak (*Quercus phellos*).

3.2.5.1.2 Wildlife

No wildlife species were observed within the study area during the December 17, 2009, site visit. The approximate 18-acre rough graded area provides no wildlife value. Common wildlife species within the region that utilize the forested habitat (lot 6) includes white-tailed deer (*Odocoileus virginianus*), red foxes (*Vulpes vulpes*), raccoons (*Procyon lotor*), squirrels (*Sciurus niger*), and various other small mammal species such as white-footed mice (*Peromyscus Leucopus*) and shrews (*Sorex sp.*). Although no habitat exists within the project site, according to the North Carolina Wildlife Resources Commission, the Carolina darter, *Erheostoma collis* (a State special concern species), is known from within Coddle Creek and its tributaries (also see Section 3.1 Surface Water).

3.2.5.2   Environmental Consequences

3.2.5.2.1   No Action Alternative

Under the No Action Alternative, plant construction and operations would not occur; therefore, no impacts would occur to vegetation and wildlife.

3.2.5.2.2   Proposed Project

Informal coordination letters have been sent to both the USFWS and the North Carolina Natural Heritage Program to verify the project would have no impact on any Federally- or State-listed threatened, endangered, or candidate species, or critical habitat within the vicinity of Celgard's Proposed Project (see Appendix A). In a letter dated January 12, 2010, the North Carolina Natural Heritage Program verified they have no record of rare species, significant natural communities, significant natural heritage areas, or conservation/managed areas at or within a mile of the project site. In addition, the letter stated the use of Natural Heritage Program data should not be substituted for actual field surveys, particularly if the project area contains suitable habitat for rare species, significant natural communities, or priority natural areas. As stated in Section 3.2.5.1, a majority of the site has been extensively disturbed by grading and the remaining 2.1 acres consists of early successional forest, which is common to the region. The potential for rare, threatened or endangered species or habitat, therefore, would be unlikely and additional surveys would not be warranted. The USWFS stated in a letter dated January 4, 2010, that their records indicate no Federally-listed species or their habitats occur on the subject site and that requirements under Section 7 of the Act are fulfilled.

Vegetation
Construction
Under Celgard's Proposed Project, a direct adverse impact would occur to vegetation from the loss of up to 2.1 acres of early successional forest. Construction activities associated with the proposed facility would require site grading and removal of vegetation in the area of lot 6, where grading has not already occurred. This vegetation community, however, would not be considered rare or of high value within the region. Overall impacts would, therefore, be minor from construction. Following construction, those areas temporarily disturbed within the entire 20.6-acre site would be either seeded or sodded with grass and maintained as grassy areas. Trees and shrubs would also be planted within the site as part of a landscape plan abiding by the business park covenant.

Although construction of the Proposed Project has the potential to cause sedimentation, impacts to offsite surface water features would be unlikely due to incorporation of sediment and erosion control features (see Section 3.1, Surface Water). Indirect impacts, therefore, to the Carolina darter would not be anticipated.

Operations
Other than maintenance of grass areas surrounding the proposed facility, operations of the facility are not anticipated to cause adverse impacts to vegetation.

Wildlife
Construction
Under Celgard's Proposed Project, an indirect adverse impact would occur to wildlife from the loss of approximately 2.1 acres of early successional forested habitat. Construction activities associated with the proposed facility would require site grading and removal of vegetation in the area of lot 6 where grading has not already occurred. Wildlife utilizing this area would likely move to similar habitat available adjacent to the site. Noise from construction activities (see Section 3.2.2) would have the potential to disturb wildlife species within proximity to the study area. Overall adverse impacts, however, would be minor as the area already contains disturbance to habitat within the project site from previous vegetation removal and rough grading.

Operations
Operation of the facility is not anticipated to create additional disturbance to wildlife other than the mowing of established grassy areas.

3.2.5.3 Cumulative Impacts

Industrial and rural farm and residential uses adjacent to the project site have caused localized and adverse disturbances to vegetation and wildlife. As the project site is located within a State- and locally-approved business park, additional disturbances would likely occur to vegetation and wildlife within the remaining undeveloped lots located in the business park as they become developed. These impacts, however, would be localized, and disturbance would occur over time. The overall adverse cumulative impacts to vegetation and wildlife would be minor.

3.2.5.4 Proposed Mitigation Measures

No mitigation measures would be required for vegetation and wildlife.

3.2.6 Socioeconomics

3.2.6.1 Affected Environment

Population and Housing
In 2008, the population of Cabarrus County was 168,740 (U.S. Census Bureau, 2008). The demographic makeup of Cabarrus County is somewhat similar to that of the State of North Carolina; however, the County has a lesser concentration of Black or African Americans, and American Indians and Alaska Natives; and a slightly higher population of Hispanic/Latino individuals. Table 3.2.6-1 provides population and demographic statistics.

Table 3.2.6-1. Population and Demographic Statistics for Cabarrus County, North Carolina

Population Group	Cabarrus County, North Carolina (2008)	North Carolina (2008)	United States (2008)
Total Population	168,740	9,222,414	304,059,724
	Percent of Total Population	**Percent of Total Population**	**Percent of Total Population**
White	81.8	73.9	79.8
Black or African American	15.1	21.6	12.8
American Indian and Alaska Native	0.4	1.3	1.0
Asian	1.6	1.9	4.5
Native Hawaiian or Other Pacific Islander	NA	0.1	0.2
Two or More Races	1.1	1.2	1.7
Hispanic/Latino Origin (any race)	8.9	7.4	15.4

Source: U.S. Census American Community Survey 2006-2008

Taxes and Revenue
The State of North Carolina levies a 6.0 percent individual income tax on incomes greater than $12,570; 7.0 percent on income between $12,750 and $60,000 (on the amount over $12,750); and 7.75 percent on income over $60,000 (on the amounts over $60,000) on residents within the state (NCDR, 2009). Cabarrus County's property tax rate is $0.63 per assessed $100 on personal and real estate property (Cabarrus County, 2009b).

Economy and Employment
The economic conditions in Cabarrus County, North Carolina are slightly different from State and national economic conditions. According to the American Community Survey, the unemployment rate between 2006 and 2008 was 7 percent in Cabarrus County, slightly higher than the State (4.3 percent) and about the same as

National levels. The per capita income for Cabarrus County is slightly higher than the State and slightly lower than the United States. The percent of individuals living in poverty in Cabarrus County was slightly lower than both the State of North Carolina and the United States. Table 3.2.6-2 provides economic statistics.

Table 3.2.6-2. Economic Statistics for Cabarrus County, North Carolina

Population Group	Cabarrus County, North Carolina (2008)	North Carolina (2008)	United States (2008)
Unemployment Rate (Percent)	7	4.3	6.6
Per Capita Income	$ 26,426	$25,015	$27,466
Median Household Income	$ 51,927	$44,772	$50,740
Individuals Below Poverty Level (Percent)	11.1	14.3	13.0

Source: U.S. Census American Community Survey 2006-2008

The industries that provide the greatest number of jobs include manufacturing, retail trade, and education. Cabarrus County employers (with 1,000 or more employees) include Cabarrus County Schools; Northeast Medical Center; Philip Morris USA, Inc.; Wal-Mart Associates, Inc.; and Cabarrus County (EDIS, 2008).

3.2.6.2   Environmental Consequences

3.2.6.2.1   No Action Alternative

Under the No Action Alternative, construction and operations would not occur; therefore, there would be no changes to socioeconomics.

3.2.6.2.2   Proposed Project

Population and Housing
Construction
During construction approximately 40 to 60 construction jobs (80 to 100 during peak construction) would be created as a result of Celgard's Proposed Project. It is assumed that the majority of the workforce would be drawn from local candidates; therefore, no increase in population or need for housing is anticipated.

Operations
Approximately 273 permanent jobs are expected to be created as a result of Celgard's Proposed Project. One of the site selection criteria for Celgard to select the Concord site was that of a qualified, available, and local workforce. Therefore, it is assumed that the majority of the workforce would be drawn from local candidates; thus, no increase in population or need for housing is anticipated. Negligible to minor impacts to housing and population are anticipated.

Taxes and Revenue
Construction
Under Celgard's Proposed Project, construction workers employed for the construction period are assumed to be currently employed, and residing and paying taxes in the Cabarrus County area. Increased sales transactions for the purchase of materials and supplies would generate some additional revenues for local and state governments, which would have a minor beneficial impact on taxes and revenue.

Operations
During operation, taxes would continue to be paid on the property and no adverse impacts to revenue would occur. Income taxes would be collected from the additional 273 employees that would exist as a result of Celgard's Proposed Project. This would have a minor beneficial impact on revenue.

Additional retail services and business employment may result from Celgard's Proposed Project through a multiplier effect, yielding additional sales and income tax revenues for local and state governments, thus having a moderate beneficial impact.

Economy and Employment
Construction
Under Celgard's Proposed Project, regional economic activity would increase as local construction contractors and construction firms are hired for the project. The purchase of building materials, construction supplies and construction equipment, as well as spending by the construction workers, would add income to the economy.

Approximately 40 to 60 construction jobs (80 to 100 during peak construction) would be created as a result of Celgard's Proposed Project. This would have a minor beneficial impact on employment in the County.

Operations
Daily spending by employees would positively affect businesses in the area. These expenditures commonly include gasoline, automobile servicing, food and beverages, laundry, and other retail purchases undertaken in the immediate area because of convenience and access during the course of the business day.

Approximately 273 permanent jobs would be created as a result of Celgard's Proposed Project. In addition, secondary jobs related to the increased economic activity stimulated by Celgard's Proposed Project may also be created. This would have a minor beneficial impact on employment in the County.

3.2.6.3   Cumulative Impacts

The proposed Celgard project would contribute to cumulative positive revenue impacts for the state, county, and local governments as associated with the historical trend of past, present, and reasonable foreseeable future activities.

3.2.6.4   Proposed Mitigation Measures

No mitigation measures are recommended for socioeconomic resources.

3.2.7   Utilities and Energy Use

3.2.7.1   Affected Environment

International Business Park, in which the Celgard Proposed Action site would be located, currently has arrangements with regional utility suppliers, as well as the required utility infrastructure, to provide utility needs for its current tenants. The property is located within the potable and wastewater service areas of the City of Concord Water System. Municipal potable water is drawn and treated by two city plants: the Coddle Creek Water Treatment Plant and the Hillgrove Water Treatment Plant. The City of Concord Water System has a total capacity to supply up to 20 million gallons per day (mgd) of potable water. Municipal wastewater is treated at the Rocky River Wastewater Treatment plant, which has a peak capacity of 24 mgd and an average capacity of 14.5 mgd (Mauldin, 2009).

The City of Concord supplies electricity to the proposed site, purchasing its power from Duke Energy. The City of Concord has an average capacity of 28.5 megawatts within their entire service area. Duke Energy is one of the largest electric power companies in the United States and has approximately 35,000 megawatts of electric generating capacity in the Midwest and the Carolinas. Piedmont Natural Gas of Charlotte, North Carolina supplies natural gas to the business park.

3.2.7.2   Environmental Consequences

3.2.7.2.1   No Action Alternative

Under the No Action Alternative, construction and operations would not occur; therefore, no impacts would occur to utilities and energy use.

3.2.7.2.2   Proposed Project

Construction

During construction for Celgard's Proposed Project, utilities would be supplied by existing services, which would not be adversely impacted by the small temporary demand.

Operations

The proposed project manufacturing process would not require any process water, nor would it discharge any process wastewater. The only water required for the facility operations would be for employee sanitary purposes. Celgard estimates the proposed facility would consume less than 9,000 gallons per day of water for human consumption and sanitary use (Celgard, 2009a). This demand would represent less than 0.1 percent of the capacity of the City of Concord Water System. Therefore, the impacts on water utilities would be negligible. Accessing the water utilities would also have minor impact as the main water supply and sewer lines currently abut the project site cul-de-sac.

The Celgard facility energy demand would only require electricity. The estimate for the new facility would be 1,700 kilowatts per hour for startup and 1,500 kilowatts per month for normal operations. The startup, anticipated of 1-month duration, would involve checking the equipment operation and the initial heating up of the equipment. Peak demand could be up to 22-23,000 kilowatts per month; however, normal operations are where the equipment has a percentage of idle status due to product changes, maintenance, and quality control. The usage is 1,500 kilowatts per month. If the facility operates at maximum utilization, the monthly usage increases to 23,000 kilowatts per month, but this would not be sustained for more than a few weeks at a time. This increased energy demand can easily be accommodated by Duke Energy, and would have only a minor impact. A substation has already been constructed in the Business Park area to handle the anticipated demands of the park's development at full capacity. Electric lines would be run underground. Celgard is seeking LEED (Leadership in Energy and Environmental Design) certification of the new facility, and would likely augment its electrical power supply with solar receptors.

Natural gas may be used at the site for heating. The existing pipeline is at the crossroad of Business Boulevard and Enterprise Drive. Natural gas would be supplied by Piedmont Natural Gas, for which a gas line would need to be run to the end of the cul-de-sac. The use of natural gas by Celgard's Proposed Project, if required, would have only a minor impact on the utility.

3.2.7.3   Cumulative Impacts

Currently, other than the proposed Celgard project, no other projects are planned. However, the project site is located within a State- and locally-approved business park; therefore, it is anticipated that with the full development of the business park, cumulative adverse impacts to utilities could occur in association with the historical trend of past, present, and reasonably foreseeable future activities.

3.2.7.4   Proposed Mitigation Measures

No mitigation would be required for utilities and energy supply.

3.2.8 Transportation and Traffic

3.2.8.1 Affected Environment

The proposed site is located within the existing International Business Park, Concord, is zoned Industrial, and is currently bordered by industrial use and warehouse space to the north and east, and residential properties to the south, west, and southeast.

The major arterial roads in the region are Interstate Highway I-85 that runs in a southwest-northeast direction approximately 0.6 miles to the west of the property; Davidson Highway (Highway 73) that runs in a west-east direction approximately 1.2 miles to the north of the site; and Warren C. Coleman Boulevard (Highway 601 Bypass) that runs in a north-south direction approximately 2.5 miles east of the site.

The site is located at the south end of Business Boulevard, its only access road. Business Boulevard intersects Enterprise Drive approximately 300 yards north of the property, and Enterprise Drive intersects International Drive approximately 300 yards to the east. Both Business Boulevard and Enterprise Drive are cul-de-sacs dedicated to serve the Business Park tenants. International Drive is the main route to access the Business Park from the north and south. Traffic may access International Drive via Davidson Highway (Highway 73) about 0.8 miles north of the Enterprise Drive intersection or from Poplar Tent Road about 0.5 miles south of the intersection. Traffic may merge onto I-85 approximately 0.2 miles to the west of the International Drive and Davidson Highway intersection.

3.2.8.2 Environmental Consequences

3.2.8.2.1 No Action Alternative

Under the No Action Alternative, plant construction and operation would not occur; therefore, no impacts would occur to transportation and traffic.

3.2.8.2.2 Proposed Project

Construction
Short-term but measurable adverse minor impacts to traffic are expected during the construction phase of the proposed facility. Site preparation and construction would include final grading of the property, construction of the main manufacturing building shell and all internal structural configurations, needed roadways and employee parking lot, commercial carrier truck access (including five truck docks), installation of utility lines, and installation of all manufacturing and other facility equipment.

The construction activities of Celgard's Proposed Project are expected to last for approximately 11 to 12 months (Celgard, 2009a). Construction vehicles and construction workers' vehicles would add to existing local traffic and would potentially cause minor congestion, higher traffic noise, and increased vehicle emission levels along the routes. Construction of Celgard's Proposed Project is expected to utilize approximately 80 to 100 workers during the three-month peak phase of construction and approximately 40 to 60 workers during the remaining eight to nine months. The personal vehicles of the construction workers would contribute to regional traffic levels primarily at the beginning and ending of the workday. The roads most impacted outside the International Business Park would be Davidson Highway and Poplar Tent Road; however, these roads adequately accommodate current industrial truck and employee vehicle traffic to and from the industrial complex. The roads within the business park (Business Boulevard, Enterprise Drive, and International Drive) have been designed to accommodate industrial or construction truck and vehicle traffic.

Operations
Celgard's Proposed Project would generate a minor long-term increase in truck and personal-vehicle traffic into and out of the International Business Park. The operations would be expected to require approximately 4 truck visits per day for deliveries and shipments, and roughly 150 personal vehicles due to the hiring of approximately 273 employees (including plant shift workers and office staff). The plant would operate 24 hours per day with

three shifts. Approximately 80 employees would work per shift (Celgard, 2009a). The trucks and vehicles would use the established road network accessing the site. This increase in traffic would have only minor impact to the surrounding community as the existing roadway and intersection network can accommodate this increase in traffic, and the facility site design would include adequate parking, loading, and maneuver space for these vehicles and trucks. Furthermore, the proposed site would be located at the end of a dedicated cul-de-sac, further reducing traffic impact to surrounding industries.

3.2.8.3   Cumulative Impacts

Currently, other than the proposed Celgard project, no other projects are planned. However, the project site is located within a State- and locally-approved business park; therefore, it is anticipated that with the full development of the business park, cumulative adverse impacts would likely occur to the local roadway network associated with the historical trend of past, present, and reasonable foreseeable future activities.

3.2.8.4   Proposed Mitigation Measures

No mitigation measures would be required for transportation and traffic.

3.2.9   Human Health and Safety

3.2.9.1   Affected Environment

The site is currently undeveloped property that has been graded to prepare the site for construction. As discussed in Section 3.1, an ESA was performed for the site and no signs of a past release are present at the site and no evidence was noted to indicate that hazardous or toxic materials are or have previously been disposed of or produced at the site (CESI, 2005).

3.2.9.2   Environmental Consequences

3.2.9.2.1   No Action Alternative

Under the No Action Alternative, construction and operations would not occur; therefore, no impacts would occur to human health and safety.

3.2.9.2.2   Proposed Project

Construction
The proposed facility would be newly constructed on a vacant lot and would not require the removal of any structures. As described in Section 3.1, no known historical releases have occurred at the site, and no evidence of historical spills is present. Construction workers would follow safety standards applicable to the construction site hazards to ensure the health and safety of workers. No impact related to health and safety would occur under Celgard's Proposed Project from construction of the facility.

Operations
The proposed facility would include a battery testing laboratory that would use alcohols, solvents, and electrolytes. The Celgard facility would have an environmental, health and safety plan to address the safe handling, storage and disposal of these materials to ensure worker health and safety. As an established operation for similar types of work at the Celgard facility in Charlotte, North Carolina, Celgard has experienced personnel who would support the project, thereby reducing the chance of accidents, spills, and leaks. Celgard employees at the existing Charlotte facility receive initial environmental safety and health training as well as regular refresher training based on job responsibilities and regulatory requirements. Production and laboratory employees require certification of job training by Celgard in accordance with ISO 9001 and ISO 14001 standards. Celgard would adopt these standards at the new facility (Celgard, 2009a). The Celgard facility located in Charlotte, North Carolina has an Environmental Health & Safety Plan in place that was most recently updated in February 2009. This plan would be modified to address health and safety issues at the new facility.

The main raw material would be polypropylene and polyethylene resins in dry pellet form, which would be stored outdoors in silos or indoors in large sacks. Small quantities of liquid solvents would be stored indoors, primarily in the laboratory. Because materials and resulting wastes would be stored on site, the potential risk of exposure would be greatest for Celgard employees, who would be trained in proper safety procedures. The risk of exposure to hazardous materials by the general population would not be expected to occur.

Because critical hourly or daily functions of strategic importance to the national economy are not reliant on plant operations, the Celgard facility is not considered a potential target for intentional destructive acts. Furthermore, the facility would not maintain sufficient quantities of materials that could threaten public health and safety in the surrounding population if released catastrophically. Although the supply of separator material could be interrupted temporarily by a destructive act, the interruption would be relatively brief and would not be expected to have lasting effects on the economy. The potential for impacts of an intentional destructive act on human health and safety would be reduced through implementation of emergency procedures to be developed by Celgard.

3.2.9.3 Cumulative Impacts

The proposed Celgard project does not appear to have manufacturing processes or products that could be involved in cumulative impacts on human health and safety, locally or nationally. No reasonably foreseeable actions have been identified that would interact with Celgard's Proposed Project to generate cumulative adverse impacts to human health and safety.

3.2.9.4 Proposed Mitigation Measures

During construction, safety measures such as providing fencing around the construction site, establishing contained storage areas, and controlling the movement of construction equipment and personnel would reduce the potential for an accident to occur. Additionally, Section 3.2.1.4 identifies proposed mitigation measures to minimize human health and safety impacts to air quality caused by fugitive dust and tailpipe emissions.

This page intentionally left blank.

4.0   REFERENCES

40 CFR 50 "National Primary and Secondary Ambient Air Quality Standards" U.S. Environmental Protection Agency, Code of Federal Regulations.

40 CFR 51.166. "Requirements for Preparation, Adoption and Submittal of Implementation Plans: Prevention of Significant Deterioration of Air Quality." U.S. Environmental Protection Agency, Code of Federal Regulations.

40 CFR 52.21. "Prevention of Significant Deterioration of Air Quality." U.S. Environmental Protection Agency, Code of Federal Regulations.

40 CFR 52.21(c). "Prevention of Significant Deterioration of Air Quality: Ambient Air Increments." U.S. Environmental Protection Agency, Code of Federal Regulations.

40 CFR 93. "Determining Conformity of Federal Actions to State or Federal Implementation Plans." U.S. Environmental Protection Agency, Code of Federal Regulations.

Arora, Pankaj and Zhengming (John) Zhang, Celgard, LLC (Arora and Zhang). 2004. *Battery Separators*, American Chemical Society Chemical Reviews, Vol. 104, No. 10. Published on the web October 13, 2004.

Cabarrus County. 2009a. Cabarrus County Noise Ordinance. Section 30-201 Enumeration of Prohibited Acts. Accessed on December 18 2009 at http://cabarruscounty.us/Jail/noise.html.

Cabarrus County. 2009b. Cabarrus County Property Tax Rates. Accessed on December 29, 2009 at http://www.co.cabarrus.nc.us/tax/rates.html.

Center for Climate Strategies (CCS). 2007. Final North Carolina Greenhouse Gas Inventory and Reference Case Projections 1990-2020, Tom Peterson, et. al. September 2007.

Celgard. 2009a. Information Provided in Support of Application to Department of Energy. [confidential]

Celgard. 2009b. Correspondence from Gerald Rumierz, Business Manager, Celgard, LLC. December 18, 2009. [confidential]

Concord Engineering & Surveying, Inc. (CESI). 2005. Report of Phase I Environmental Site Assessment for International Business Park – Lots 7 and 8, Business Boulevard, Concord, North Carolina. Prepared for Cabarrus County EDC, 2325 Concord Lake Road, Concord, NC. March 25, 2005.

DOE. 1999. Department of Energy, GREET 1.5 Transportation Fuel-Cycle Mode. Accessed on November 7, 2009 at the U.S. Department of Energy - Energy Efficiency and Renewable Energy, Alternative Fuels and Advanced Vehicles Data Center: http://www.afdc.energy.gov/afdc/vehicles/emissions_electricity.html (last updated August 6, 2009).

DOE. 2001. Department of Energy, Office of Advanced Automotive Technologies. FY2001 Progress Report for the Electric Vehicle Battery Research and Development Program, December 2001, Washington, DC.

EPA. 2009a. National Ambient Air Quality Standards (NAAQS). Accessed October 31, 2009 at http://epa.gov/air/criteria.html (last updated July 14, 2009).

EPA. 2009b. The Green Book Nonattainment Areas for Criteria Pollutants. Accessed October 31, 2009 at http://www.epa.gov/oar/oaqps/greenbk/index.html (last updated October 8, 2009).

EPA. 2009c. EPA. 2009. NEPAssist. Superfund Site Layer – Concord, North Carolina Search. http://epamap9.epa.gov/nepave/nepamap.aspx?action=searchloc&wherestr=for%20International%20Business%20Park%20Business%20Boulevard%2C%20Concord%2C%20North%20Carolina.%20%20). Accessed December 16, 2009.

EPA. 2009d. NEPAssist. Wetland Inventory and Floodplain Data Layers – Concord, North Carolina Site Accessed December 21, 2009 at http://epamap9.epa.gov/nepave/nepamap.aspx?action=openses&p_nepaid=10473020091217FCARE.

Huffman, R.L. 1996. *Ground Water in the Piedmont and Blue Ridge Provinces of North Carolina.* March 1996. North Carolina Cooperative Extension Service. Publication# AG 473-6. Accessed December 22, 2009 at http://www.bae.ncsu.edu/programs/extension/publicat/wqwm/ag473_6/.

LeGrand, Sr., H.E. 2004. A Master Conceptual Model for Hydrogeological Site Characterization in the Piedmont and Mountain Region of North Carolina – A Guidance Manual. North Carolina Department of Environment and Natural Resources, Division of Water Quality, Groundwater Section. Accessed December 22, 2009 at http://h2o.enr.state.nc.us/gwp/Acrobat%20docs/legrand_04.pdf.

NCSU. 2009. State Climate Office of North Carolina, Weather and Climate. Accessed at http://www.nc-climate.ncsu.edu/products/wx.

North Carolina Department of Environment and Natural Resources (NCDENR). 2009. NCDENR, Division of Air Quality, Air Pollution Control Requirement: Section 0400-Ambient Air Quality Standards. Accessed October 31, 2009 at http://daq.state.nc.us/rules/rules/Sec0400.shtml (last updated October 29, 2009).

North Carolina Department of Revenue (NCDR). 2009. North Carolina Department of Revenue Tax Rates. Accessed on December 29, 2009 at http://www.dornc.com/taxes/individual/rates.html.

North Carolina Division of Water Quality (NC DWQ). 2008. *Yadkin-Pee Dee River Basin Plan 2008.* Accessed December 22, 2009 at http://h2o.enr.state.nc.us/basinwide/Neuse/2008/documents/Yadkin-PeeDeeBasinPlan2008printjob.pdf.

NC DWQ. 2009. *2008 North Carolina Draft Integrated Report Category 5 (303(d) list).* Accessed December 22, 2009 at http://h2o.enr.state.nc.us/tmdl/documents/PartBdraft2008IRCat5.pdf.

NPS, 2009a. National Park Service, Class I Area Location. Accessed November 2, 2009 at http://www.nature.nps.gov/air/Maps/classILoc.cfm (last updated December 16, 2007).

NPS, 2009b. National Park Service, Permit Application, PSD Overview. Accessed November 2, 2009 at http://www.nature.nps.gov/air/permits/index.cfm (last updated March 28, 2006).

NRIS, 2009. National Register of Historic Places Database. Accessed at http://www.nps.gov/history/nr/research/nris.htm on December 2009.

NRCS. 2009. National Resource Conservation Service. Cabarrus County Soil Survey. Version 10, May 28, 2009. Accessed December 21, 2009 at http://websoilsurvey.nrcs.usda.gov (last updated December 21, 2009).

SERCC, 2009. Southeast Regional Climate Center, Shelby, North Carolina (317845) Period of Record Monthly Climate Summary. Accessed December 30, 2009 at http://www.sercc.com/cgi-bin/sercc/cliMAIN.pl?nc1975 (last updated April 30, 2009).

5.0 LIST OF PREPARERS

Department of Energy	
Bruce Mixer	Project Manager
Mark McKoy	NEPA Document Manager
Jesse Garcia	NEPA Document Manager
Celgard LLC	
Gerald Rumierz	Project Manager
Charlie Steenrod	Engineering Manager
Gerry Palmer	Environmental Health and Safety Manager

PHE		
Analyst	**Responsibilites**	**Degrees and Experience**
Anthony Becker	Technical Writer: Surface Water, Groundwater, Wetlands and Floodplains	M.S., Biology B.S., Biology 5 years experience, 5 years NEPA experience
Frederick Carey, P.E.	Senior Engineer, QA/QC	M.S., Environmental Engineering B.S., Civil Engineering 17 years experience, 17 years NEPA experience
Austina Casey	Technical Writer: Air Quality and Climate	M.S., Environmental Science and Policy B.S., Chemistry 18 years experience, 6 years NEPA experience
Angela Drum	Senior Word Processor	10 years experience, 5 years NEPA experience
Joseph Grieshaber	QA/QC	M.B.A., Finance M.S., Biology B.S., Biology 34 years experience, 21 years NEPA experience
Robin Griffin	Assistant Project Manager, Technical Writer: Socioeconomics, Environmental Justice, Cultural	M.S., Environmental Management B.A., English Composition 17 years experience, 15 years NEPA experience
Jamie Martin-McNaughton	Sharepoint Administrator	B.S., Geology-Biology 7 years experience, 5 years NEPA experience
Robert Naumann	Technical Writer: Natural Resources, Geology and Soils	B.S., Natural Resources M.S., Environmental Science 11 years experience, 11 years NEPA experience
Deborah Shinkle	GIS Specialist	B.A., Environmental Studies 6 years experience, 5 years NEPA experience
Rachel Spangenberg	Technical Writer: Materials and Waste Management	B.S., Biology 20 years experience, 15 years NEPA experience
Debra Walker	Project Manager	B.S., Biology 33 years experience, 20 years NEPA experience
Andrea Wilkes	Technical Writer: Noise, Traffic and Transportation	M.A., Science Writing B.S., Civil and Environmental Engineering B.S., English Literature 24 years experience, 2 years NEPA experience

This page intentionally left blank.

6.0   DISTRIBUTION LIST

Ms. Renee Gledhill-Earley
Environmental Review Coordinator
North Carolina State Historic Preservation Office
4610 Mail Service Center
Raleigh NC 27699-4610

Ms. Chrys Baggett
North Carolina Department of Administration
State Environmental Review Clearinghouse
1301 Mail Service Center
Raleigh, NC 27699-1301

Head Librarian
Cabarrus County Public Library
Concord Branch
27 Union Street, N
Concord, NC 28025

Mr. W. Brian Hiatt
Concord City Manager
P.O. Box 309
Concord, NC 28026-0308

Mr. Harry E. Legrand, Jr.
Zoologist
North Carolina Natural Heritage Program
1601 Mail Service Center
Raleigh, NC 27699-1601

Mr. Ron Linville, Regional Coordinator
North Carolina Wildlife Resources Commission
Division of Inland Fisheries
1721 Mail Service Center
Raleigh, NC 27699-1721

Ms. Valerie W. McMillian
Director, State Environmental Policy Act
North Carolina Department of Administration
1301 Mail Service Center
Raleigh, NC 27699-1301

Mr. Jim McRight
Department of Environment and Natural Resources
Division of Environmental Health
Mooresville Regional Office
610 East Center Avenue, Suite 301
Mooresville, NC 28115

Mr. John J. Mintz
Assistant State Archaeologist
4619 Mail Service Center
Raleigh, NC 27699-4619

Mr. Heinz Mueller
Chief of NEPA Program Office
U.S. Environmental Protection Agency Region 4
61 Forsyth Street, SW
Atlanta, GA 30303

Mayor J. Scott Padgett
Mayor, City of Concord
P.O. Box 309
Concord, NC 28026-0308

Honorable Beverly Perdue
Governor of North Carolina
Office of the Governor
20301 Mail Service Center
Raleigh, NC 27699-0301

Mr. Allen Ratzlaff
U.S. Fish and Wildlife Service
Asheville Ecological Services Field Office
160 Zillicoa Street
Asheville, NC 28801-1082

Britt Setzer-Moorsville RO
Department of Environment and Natural Resources
Division of Environmental Health
Mooresville Regional Office
610 East Center Avenue, Suite 301
Mooresville, NC 28115

This page intentionally left blank.

Appendix A

Agency Consultation

This page intentionally left blank.

Appendix B

Public Comments on the Draft Environmental Assessment and Responses from the Department of Energy and Celgard LLC

This page intentionally left blank.